I0789562

GUINEA-BISSAU

GUINEA-BISSAU

GUINEA-BISSAU 2016 HUMAN RIGHTS REPORT

EXECUTIVE SUMMARY

Guinea-Bissau is a multiparty republic. It is ruled by a democratically elected government led by President Jose Mario Vaz and Prime Minister Baciro Dja of the African Party for the Independence of Guinea and Cabo Verde (PAIGC). Vaz took office in 2014 after an election judged to be free and fair by international observers. The country has endured prolonged PAIGC intraparty political turmoil since the August 2015 dismissal of Prime Minister Domingos Simoes Pereira and the subsequent dismissal on May 12 of Pereira's successor, Carlos Correia.

Unlike in prior years, the government maintained civilian authority over the security forces.

Serious human rights abuses included arbitrary detention; official corruption exacerbated by government officials' impunity and suspected involvement in drug trafficking; and violence and discrimination against women and children.

Other human rights abuses included abusive treatment of detainees; poor conditions of detention; lack of judicial independence and due process; interference with privacy; female genital mutilation/cutting (FGM/C); and trafficking in persons.

The government did not take effective steps to prosecute or punish officials or other individuals who committed abuses, whether in the security services or elsewhere in the government. Impunity was a serious problem.

Section 1. Respect for the Integrity of the Person, Including Freedom from:

a. Arbitrary Deprivation of Life and other Unlawful or Politically Motivated Killings

There were no reports the government or its agents committed arbitrary or unlawful killings.

b. Disappearance

There were no reports of politically motivated disappearances.

c. Torture and Other Cruel, Inhuman, or Degrading Treatment or Punishment

The constitution and law prohibit such practices. Unlike in prior years, the armed forces and police respected these prohibitions.

Prison and Detention Center Conditions

Prison conditions varied widely. In the makeshift detention facilities for pretrial detainees, conditions were harsh and life threatening. Except in the prisons in Bafata and Mansoa, electricity, potable water, and space were inadequate.

Physical Conditions: Conditions of confinement were poor. Detention facilities generally lacked secure cells, running water, adequate heating, ventilation, lighting, and sanitation. Detainees' diets were poor, and medical care was virtually nonexistent. At the pretrial detention center in Bissau, detainees relied on their families for food. Officials held pretrial detainees with convicted prisoners and juveniles with adults.

Administration: Authorities did not maintain adequate records or investigate allegations of inhuman conditions. In many cases authorities released detainees informally on their own recognizance or simply allowed them to walk away from makeshift detention facilities. There was no prison ombudsman to respond to prisoners' complaints or independent authorities to investigate credible allegations of inhuman conditions.

Independent Monitoring: The government permitted independent monitoring of detention conditions by local and international human rights groups. According to the Justice Ministry's director of justice administration, the UN Integrated Peacebuilding Office in Guinea-Bissau and the National Commission for Human Rights regularly visited the prisons in Mansoa and Bafata.

d. Arbitrary Arrest or Detention

The constitution and law prohibit arbitrary arrest and detention, and the government usually observed these prohibitions.

Role of the Police and Security Apparatus

The country is divided into 37 police districts. An estimated 3,500 police personnel in nine different police forces reported to seven different ministries. The Judicial Police, under the Ministry of Justice, has primary responsibility for investigating drug trafficking, terrorism, and other transnational crimes. The Public Order Police, under the Ministry of Interior, is responsible for preventive patrols, crowd control, and maintenance of law and order. Other police forces include the State Information Service (intelligence), Border Police (migration and border enforcement), Rapid Intervention Police, and Maritime Police. According to the constitution, the armed forces are responsible for external security and may be called upon to assist police in emergencies.

Police were generally ineffective, poorly and irregularly paid, and corrupt. They received no training and had insufficient funding to buy fuel for police vehicles. Traffic police often demanded bribes from vehicle drivers, whether or not their documents and vehicles were in order. Lack of police detention facilities frequently resulted in prisoners leaving custody during investigations. Impunity was a serious problem. The attorney general was responsible for investigating police abuses; however, employees of that office were also poorly paid and susceptible to threats, corruption, and coercion.

A military court system exists, with the Supreme Military Court as the final court of appeal for military cases. Although civilian courts could try cases involving state security personnel, they were reluctant to assert jurisdiction over members of the military.

Arrest Procedures and Treatment of Detainees

The law requires arrest warrants, although warrantless arrests often occurred, particularly of immigrants suspected of crimes. By law detainees must be brought before a magistrate within 48 hours after arrest and be released if no indictment is filed; however, authorities did not always respect these rights. Authorities generally informed detainees of charges against them, although this was not always the case for military detainees. Although the law provides for the right to counsel at state expense for indigent clients, lawyers did not receive compensation for their part-time public defense work and often ignored state directives to represent indigent clients. There was a functioning bail system but no alternatives for considering release pending trial. Pretrial detainees had prompt access to family members. Civilian suspects were usually held under house arrest.

<u>Arbitrary Arrest</u>: There were reports police occasionally arrested persons arbitrarily and detained them without due process.

<u>Detainee's Ability to Challenge Lawfulness of Detention before a Court</u>: Detainees may challenge the lawfulness of detention before a court through a regular appeals process, obtain prompt release, and obtain compensation if found to have been unlawfully detained; provisions for compensation were rarely enforced, however. For example, in August the attorney for Joao Bernardo Vieira successfully argued that he was improperly detained for failure to appear before the attorney general. The court ordered Vieira's release based on evidence that he was not notified in advance to appear before the attorney general.

e. Denial of Fair Public Trial

The constitution and law provide for an independent judiciary, but the judiciary had little independence and was subject to significant political manipulation. Judges were poorly trained, inadequately and irregularly paid, and subject to corruption. Courts and judicial authorities were also frequently biased and unproductive. The attorney general was subject to political pressure. A lack of resources and infrastructure often delayed trials, and convictions were extremely rare. Authorities respected court orders, however.

On April 5, the Supreme Court ruled that the National Assembly's December 2015 expulsion of 15 PAIGC parliamentarians, following their refusal to vote for the government's program, was unconstitutional. The 15 parliamentarians were subsequently reinstated. On June 8, the Supreme Court ruled the second government of Prime Minister Baciro Dja was legal and President Jose Mario Vaz complied with constitutional requirements when he dismissed the government of Carlos Correia and replaced it with that of Dja. In both cases all parties accepted the court's decision.

Trial Procedures

Citizens have the right to a presumption of innocence; to be informed promptly of the charges, with free interpretation as necessary, from the moment charged through all appeals; to a fair trial without undue delay; to be present at their trial; and to communicate with an attorney of choice or have one provided at court expense from the moment charged and through all appeals. The law provides for the right to access evidence held by the government, to confront witnesses and present witnesses and evidence, not to be compelled to testify against oneself or to admit guilt, and to appeal. Defendants generally have adequate time and facilities to prepare a defense; however, most cases never came to trial. There is no trial by jury. Trials in civilian courts are open to the public.

Authorities generally respected these rights in the few cases that went to trial. Court-appointed attorneys, however, were not punished for failing to represent indigent clients, and generally ignored such responsibilities.

Political Prisoners and Detainees

There was one opposition political detainee in detention at year's end. On July 28, judicial police arrested National Assembly Deputy Gabriel Sow, a prominent intra-PAIGC opponent, on corruption charges, despite the constitutional immunity from prosecution he had as a member of parliament. The PAIGC issued a statement calling Sow's arrest a case of unconstitutional political harassment directed by President Vaz. Sow appealed the legality of his arrest to the Court of Appeal. The court denied the appeal. It ruled that Sow did not have immunity because the corruption charge was filed before he entered parliament. During Sow's arrest and detention, he was afforded the same protections as other prisoners and government authorities permitted access by humanitarian organizations such as the International Committee of the Red Cross. Sow remained in detention at year's end.

Civil Judicial Procedures and Remedies

Individuals may seek civil remedies for human rights violations; however, there was no specific administrative mechanism to address human rights violations, and domestic court orders pertaining to human rights were not always enforced.

f. Arbitrary or Unlawful Interference with Privacy, Family, Home, or Correspondence

The constitution and law prohibit such actions, but the government did not always respect these prohibitions. Police routinely ignored privacy rights and protections against unreasonable search and seizure. For example, on January 31, PAIGC party spokesperson Joao Bernardo Vieira's home was burgled and a cache of personal papers removed; allegedly political harassment by operatives of the president. On August 17, judicial police acting on orders from the Attorney General's Office, but without an arrest warrant, forcibly entered the Vieira residence and arrested him. He was taken to police headquarters and released.

Section 2. Respect for Civil Liberties, Including:

a. Freedom of Speech and Press

The constitution and law provide for freedom of speech and press; however, there were reports the government did not always respect these rights. For example, upon his appointment in June as prime minister, Baciro Dja fired the heads of state-owned television and radio. On June 9, the dismissed head of the state-owned radio stated his dismissal was politically motivated and filed a lawsuit seeking its annulment. The case was pending at year's end. There were reports of journalists receiving threats and practicing self-censorship.

Press and Media Freedoms: There were several private newspapers in addition to the government-owned newspaper *No Pintcha*, but the state-owned printing house published all of them.

In May the country's leading pro-opposition blog *Ditadura do Consenso* was hacked. Critics accused the government of responsibility as part of its efforts to impede criticism and stifle freedom of speech. On July 7, the state-owned radio station's general manager fired his news director and editor-in-chief for having disregarded an order not to broadcast a press conference by PAIGC Chairman Domingos Simoes Pereira, one of the president's main political opponents.

Violence and Harassment: The government took no steps to preserve the safety and independence of media or to prosecute individuals who threatened journalists. For example, following firings at the state-owned radio station, a private radio station called Capital FM broadcast a program in which callers discussed and debated the dismissals. Capital FM's director subsequently received several anonymous, written death threats.

Internet Freedom

The government did not restrict or disrupt access to the internet or censor online content, and there were no credible reports the government monitored private online communications without appropriate legal authority. There were allegations, however, that on May 21, a pro-Vaz hacker succeeded in breaking into the country's leading pro-opposition blog *Ditadura do Consenso*.

According to the International Telecommunication Union, 3.54 percent of the population used the internet in 2015. Lack of infrastructure, equipment, and education severely limited access to the internet.

Academic Freedom and Cultural Events

There were no government restrictions on academic freedom or cultural events.

b. Freedom of Peaceful Assembly and Association

The constitution and law provide for the freedoms of assembly and association, and the government generally respected these rights.

c. Freedom of Religion

See the Department of State's *International Religious Freedom Report* at www.state.gov/religiousfreedomreport/.

d. Freedom of Movement, Internally Displaced Persons, Protection of Refugees, and Stateless Persons

The constitution and law provide for freedom of internal movement, foreign travel, emigration, and repatriation, and the government generally respected these rights. The government cooperated with the Office of the UN High Commissioner for Refugees (UNHCR) and other humanitarian organizations in providing protection and assistance to internally displaced persons, refugees, asylum seekers, stateless persons, and other persons of concern.

Protection of Refugees

As of February UNHCR reported the country hosted more than 8,600 Senegalese refugees and asylum seekers; most were from Senegal's Casamance Region, where a low-level separatist conflict has gone on for decades.

Some refugees from Casamance lived in Guinea-Bissau for decades, but UNHCR reported the de facto ceasefire in Senegal prompted some to return to their villages in Senegal. Other Senegalese refugees moved back and forth across the border. With ethnic and family ties on both sides of the poorly marked border, the nationality of residents along the border was not always clear.

<u>Access to Asylum</u>: The law provides for granting of asylum or refugee status, but the government system for providing protection to refugees was inactive. The government did not grant refugee status or asylum during the year, and there were no reported requests for either. The UNHCR office in Bissau facilitated the issuance of refugee cards.

<u>Durable Solutions</u>: Nearly 3,000 Senegalese refugees in 2014 told UNHCR and the country's National Commission for Refugees and Displaced Persons they wished to remain in the country permanently, and the government adopted a welcoming policy toward them. The government offered these refugees the option of citizenship or permanent residence; the first tranche was granted citizenship in 2015.

Section 3. Freedom to Participate in the Political Process

The constitution and law provide citizens with the ability to choose their government in free, fair, and periodic elections based on universal and equal suffrage and conducted by secret ballot, and in 2014 citizens exercised that ability. In the past this ability was often impeded by military intervention--as with the 2012 coup--and by corruption and bribery within political parties.

Elections and Political Participation

<u>Recent Elections</u>: The 2014 elections and the subsequent transition to a democratically elected government led by Jose Mario Vaz and Prime Minister Domingos Simoes Pereira marked a return to rule of law. With strong support from the United Nations, international observers assessed the elections as free and fair, with no credible indications of voter fraud. PAIGC candidate Vaz won a runoff with a decisive majority; the PAIGC also won a majority of seats in the National Assembly.

<u>Participation of Women and Minorities</u>: Women suffer from discrimination flowing from traditional attitudes and practices, particularly in rural areas, that discouraged them from participating in political life on the same basis as men. The 102-member National Assembly had 14 female members. Five of the 16 cabinet ministers were women, including the minister of defense. Women's groups proposed legislation providing for women to have 40 percent of seats in the National Assembly, but no progress toward passage was made during the year, due to political gridlock.

All ethnic groups were represented in the government; ethnicity was not a significant factor outside the military.

Section 4. Corruption and Lack of Transparency in Government

The law provides criminal penalties of one month to 10 years in prison for official corruption; however, the government did not implement the law effectively, and officials in all branches and on all levels of government engaged in corrupt and nontransparent practices with impunity. The World Bank's *2015 Worldwide Governance Indicators* reflected that corruption was a severe problem.

Police are mandated to fight corruption but were ineffective and received minimal external assistance or support.

The Office of the Attorney General arrested and jailed two former officials of the previous two governments during the year. Critics argued the action was not to combat corruption but was politically motivated.

Corruption: Members of the military and civilian administration reportedly trafficked in drugs and assisted international drug cartels by providing access to the country and its transportation infrastructure. The failure to interdict or investigate suspected narcotics traffickers contributed to the perception of government and military involvement in narcotics trafficking.

Financial Disclosure: By law public officials are required to disclose their personal finances before the Court of Audits and these disclosures are to be made public. The court has no authority to enforce compliance, and no penalties are specified for noncompliance. To date no public officials have disclosed their personal finances.

Public Access to Information: The law states that "everyone has the right to information" on laws, regulations, and government policies, and provides for a narrow list of exceptions, a reasonably short timeline, reasonable processing fees, administrative sanctions for noncompliance, and an appeal mechanism. Due to a lack of technical support and functioning infrastructure, authorities seldom met this requirement.

Section 5. Governmental Attitude Regarding International and Nongovernmental Investigation of Alleged Violations of Human Rights

A number of domestic and international human rights groups generally operated without government restriction, investigating and publishing their findings on human rights cases. Government officials were somewhat cooperative and responsive to their views.

Government Human Rights Bodies: The National Commission on Human Rights is a government human rights organization. It was independent but remained inadequately funded and ineffective.

Section 6. Discrimination, Societal Abuses, and Trafficking in Persons

Women

Rape and Domestic Violence: The law prohibits rape, including spousal rape, and provides penalties for conviction of two to six years in prison; however, the government did not effectively enforce the law. The law permits prosecution of rape only when reported by the victim, which observers noted was rare due to victims' fear of social stigma and retribution. This problem was exacerbated in the predominantly Muslim and ethnically Fula rural eastern regions of Gabu and Bafata, where the culture dictates the resolution of such problems within the family and community. There were no statistics available on the number of abusers prosecuted, convicted, or punished for rape.

Domestic violence, including wife beating, was widespread. No law prohibits domestic violence. Although police intervened in domestic disputes if requested, the government did not undertake specific measures to counter social pressure against reporting domestic violence, rape, incest, and other mistreatment of women.

Female Genital Mutilation/Cutting (FGM/C): The law prohibits FGM/C. Conviction of the practice is punishable by a fine of up to five million CFA francs ($8,500) and five years in prison. Muslim preachers and scholars have called for the eradication of FGM/C. The Joint Program on FGM/C of the UN Population Fund (UNFPA) and the UN Children's Fund (UNICEF) worked with the Ministry of Justice to strengthen the dissemination and application of the law by building the capacities of officials responsible for program implementation.

Among certain ethnic groups, especially the Fula and Mandinka, FGM/C was performed on girls from as young as age four months to adolescence. The 2014 *UNICEF Multiple Indicator Cluster Surveys* (MICS) reported 50 percent of girls and women ages 15-49 and 30 percent of girls ages 10-15 in the country underwent the procedure from 2002 through 2014.

In 2014, 54 percent of public health-care facilities integrated FGM/C prevention into prenatal, neonatal, and immunization services. The Ministry of Health validated and disseminated the Manual for Norms, Procedure, and Protocols on Reproductive Health in connection with FGM/C and integrated FGM/C into two other key documents, the *Strategic Plan for the Elimination of Obstetric Fistula* and the *Peer Educators' Manual on Reproductive Health.*

Sexual Harassment: There is no law prohibiting sexual harassment, and it was widespread. The government undertook no initiatives to combat the problem.

Reproductive Rights: Couples and individuals have the right to decide the number, spacing, and timing of children, free from discrimination, coercion, or violence, but they often lacked the information and means to do so. The UNFPA reported 114 health centers offered family planning services but that the availability of birth control services offered varied from center to center. The 2014 MICS reported 14.4 percent of girls and women ages 15-49 used a modern method of contraception. The Roman Catholic Church and other religious groups discouraged use of modern contraception.

According to UN estimates, the maternal mortality rate was 560 deaths per 100,000 live births in 2014, and the lifetime risk of maternal death was one in 36. Major factors causing high maternal mortality were poor health infrastructure and service delivery as well as high rates of adolescent pregnancy. The health system's obstetric care capacity was low, and emergency care was available only in Bissau. Emergency health care was available for the management of complications arising from abortion only in Bissau, which had the only two functioning hospitals in the country. Skilled health-care providers attended 93 percent of pregnant women at least once during pregnancy; however, skilled health-care workers attended only 44 percent of live births.

Discrimination: By law women have the same legal status and rights as men, but discrimination against women was a problem, particularly in rural areas where traditional and Islamic laws dominated. Women experienced discrimination in employment and pay, obtaining credit, and owning or managing businesses. Although urban women may manage land and inherit property, rural women in certain ethnic groups could do neither. Women performed most work on subsistence farms.

Children

Birth Registration: Citizenship is derived by birth within the country or from citizen parents. Birth registration does not occur automatically at hospitals; parents must register births with a notary. The government suspended collection of fees for registration in 2014 in an effort to improve compliance. The 2014 MICS indicated only 24 percent of children were registered before age five. Lack of registration resulted in denial of public services, including education, although authorities generally waived the requirement of a birth certificate at the primary school level. During the year UNICEF supported the Ministries of Health and Justice in establishing birth registration facilities in six hospitals around the country as well as in the Bissau-based national immunization center.

Education: Most children remained at home because schools were rarely open. Higher education did not function during the year. Even when schools were open, children in rural areas lacked educational opportunities because they often worked in family subsistence farming. Some children were partially or completely withdrawn from school to work in the fields during the annual cashew harvest.

Child Abuse: Violence against children was widespread but seldom reported to authorities. During the year a working group comprised of social workers from the Ministries of Health, Justice, and Women and Children updated a 2012 agreement to address sexual abuse of minors to clarify the respective roles and financial responsibilities of the three ministries in handling these cases.

Early and Forced Marriage: The legal minimum age of marriage is 17. According to UNICEF, 7 percent of girls were married or in a union before age 15. Early and forced marriage occurred among all ethnic groups. Girls who fled arranged marriages often were trafficked into commercial sex. The buying and selling of child brides also occurred. There were no government efforts to mitigate the problem. Organizations such as the Millennium Development Goals Achievement Fund worked to provide legal, social, medical, and educational services to fight child marriage and protect its victims in some locations. Working with the NGO Tostan, 157 communities have publically declared their abandonment of child marriage since 2012. Tostan implemented its Community Empowerment Program of education and engagement on child marriage and other harmful traditional practices in partnership with the government, UNICEF, the UNFPA, and local NGOs.

<u>Female Genital Mutilation/Cutting (FGM/C)</u>: Information on FGM/C is provided in the Women's section above.

<u>Sexual Exploitation of Children</u>: There is a statutory rape law prohibiting sex with a person under age 16. The rape law carries a penalty for conviction of two to six years in prison. There is no law against child pornography. When pedophilia and sexual harassment were reported, police typically blamed victims. Many families hid sexual abuse within the family to avoid shame and stigma.

Poverty led many parents to send their children to live with family members or acquaintances who could provide an education or better living conditions. Children in such situations often were vulnerable to rape, abuse, and exploitation.

<u>Displaced Children</u>: The national NGO Association of the Friends of Children estimated that up to 500 children, mostly from neighboring Guinea, lived on the streets of urban centers including Bissau, Bafata, and Gabu. The government provided no services to street children.

<u>International Child Abductions</u>: The country is not a party to the 1980 Hague Convention on the Civil Aspects of International Child Abduction. See the Department of State's *Annual Report on International Parental Child Abduction* at <u>travel.state.gov/content/childabduction/en/legal/compliance.html</u>.

Anti-Semitism

There was no known Jewish community in the country and no reports of anti-Semitic acts.

Trafficking in Persons

See the Department of State's *Trafficking in Persons Report* at <u>www.state.gov/j/tip/rls/tiprpt/</u>.

Persons with Disabilities

The law does not specifically prohibit discrimination against persons with physical, sensory, intellectual, and mental disabilities in employment, education, air travel and other transportation, access to health care, the judicial system, or other provision of state services. The government did not counter discrimination against persons with disabilities or provide access to buildings, information, and communications. The government made some efforts to assist military veterans with disabilities through pension programs, but these programs did not adequately address health care, housing, or food needs. Provisions existed to allow blind and illiterate voters to participate in the electoral process, but voters with intellectual disabilities could be restricted from voting.

Acts of Violence, Discrimination, and Other Abuses Based on Sexual Orientation and Gender Identity

There are no laws that criminalize sexual orientation. Antidiscrimination laws do not apply to lesbian, gay, bisexual, transgender, or intersex individuals. There were no reported violent incidents or other human rights abuses targeting individuals based on their sexual orientation or identity. There was no official discrimination based on sexual orientation or gender identity in employment or access to education and health care. According to government guidelines for civil servants' housing allowances, only heterosexual married couples qualified for family-size housing, while same-sex couples received the single person allotment. Social taboos against homosexuality sometimes restricted freedom to express sexual orientation, yet society was relatively tolerant of consensual same-sex conduct, according to a 2010 study by the Pew Research Center.

Section 7. Worker Rights

a. Freedom of Association and the Right to Collective Bargaining

The law provides all workers the freedom to form and join independent unions without prior authorization.

The law does not provide for the right to bargain collectively; however, the tripartite National Council for Social Consultation conducted collective consultations on salary issues. Workers and employers established most wages in bilateral negotiations.

The law provides for the right to strike, but workers must give prior notice. The law also prohibits retaliation against strikers and does not exclude any group of workers from relevant legal protections. Virtually every sector of the formal economy was on strike at some time during the year, typically for four to six weeks, usually regarding low salaries. Workers in the education, health, and public sectors struck repeatedly during the year.

The law allows unions to conduct their activities without government interference. Laws on unions provide protection only for trade union delegates, while the constitution provides for workers' rights to free speech and assembly. The law prohibits employer discrimination against official trade union representatives. The law requires reinstatement of workers terminated for union activity; there were no reports of such termination during the year.

The government was ineffective, poorly equipped, undertrained, and inadequately resourced. It did not effectively enforce applicable labor laws, including remedies and penalties. Penalties for violations, which usually took the form of fines, were insufficient to deter violations. Authorities generally respected freedom of association. No workers alleged antiunion discrimination. Worker organizations were not independent of government and political parties, employers, or employer associations, which sometimes sought to influence union decisions and actions.

b. Prohibition of Forced or Compulsory Labor

The law prohibits all forms of forced or compulsory labor, but the government did not effectively enforce the laws. Penalties, which usually took the form of fines, were sufficiently stringent and commensurate with other serious crimes such as rape, but the government did not use these or other relevant laws to prosecute cases of forced labor. There were reports forced child labor occurred, including forced begging, selling food on urban streets, and domestic service (see section 7.c.). The extent to which forced adult labor occurred was unclear, although the International Trade Union Confederation has previously called the practice of forced labor in the country an "alarming problem."

Also see the Department of State's *Trafficking in Persons Report* at www.state.gov/j/tip/rls/tiprpt/.

c. Prohibition of Child Labor and Minimum Age for Employment

There are no specific laws that protect children from hazardous occupations. The legal minimum age is 14 for general factory labor and 18 for heavy or dangerous labor, including labor in mines. Minors are prohibited from working overtime, but there were reports the practice occurred.

The Ministries of Justice and of Civil Service and Labor and the Institute of Women and Children did not effectively enforce these requirements, particularly in informal work settings. Resources, inspections, and remedies were inadequate.

Penalties usually took the form of fines and were insufficient to deter violations. The government provided no services of any kind and did not arrest or prosecute any violators.

Forced child labor occurred in domestic service; begging, including that perpetrated by corrupt teachers in some Quranic schools; agriculture and mining; shoe shining; and selling food on urban streets. Some religious teachers, known as marabouts, deceived boys and their families by promising a Quranic education but then put the boys to work or took them to neighboring countries for exploitation. The small formal sector generally adhered to minimum age requirements, although there were reports minors worked overtime despite the prohibition.

The national NGO Association of the Friends of Children is the main organization in the country working to receive and reintegrate returning "talibes," Quranic students who in some cases were trafficked into Senegal and forced to beg there. The association receives 5,770,000 CFA francs ($9,800) in government funds annually. In June, Senegalese authorities launched a campaign to eliminate forced child begging from the streets of Dakar, which significantly increased the number of talibes returning to Guinea-Bissau during the second half of the year. As of December 1, the association reported that it had received 106 talibes returning from Senegal in its Bafata-based transit center.

According to the MICS, almost 60 percent of children ages five to 14 worked, 65 percent in rural areas and 45 percent in urban areas. Children in rural communities performed domestic and fieldwork without pay to help support their families.

The government ratified the Optional Protocol to the Rights of the Child on the involvement of children in armed conflict in 2014 but undertook no investigative or enforcement actions. The Child Code bans child trafficking and provides for three to 10 years' imprisonment for conviction of the crime.

Also see the Department of Labor's *Findings on the Worst Forms of Child Labor* at www.dol.gov/ilab/reports/child-labor/findings/.

d. Discrimination with Respect to Employment and Occupation

The law and regulations do not prohibit discrimination regarding race, color, sex, religion, political opinion, national origin, citizenship, disability, language, sexual orientation or gender identity, age, HIV-positive status or having other communicable diseases, or social origin.

Women faced considerable pay gaps and, because employers preferred to avoid paying maternity benefits, were less likely to be hired than men. Documented discrimination on the other above categories with respect to employment and occupation was not available.

e. Acceptable Conditions of Work

The Council of Ministers annually establishes minimum wage rates for all categories of work. The lowest monthly wage in the formal sector was 19,030 CFA francs ($33) per month plus a bag of rice. The informal sector included an estimated 80 percent of workers. No official estimate for the poverty income level was available.

The law provides for a maximum 45-hour workweek. The law also provides for overtime work with premium pay, and overtime may not exceed 200 hours per year. There is a mandatory 12-hour rest period between workdays. The law provides for paid annual holidays.

In cooperation with unions, the Ministries of Justice and Labor establish legal health and safety standards for workers, which the National Assembly may adopt into law. The standards are current and appropriate for the main industries. Workers, including foreign workers, do not have the right to remove themselves from unsafe working conditions without losing their jobs.

The inspector general of labor is responsible for enforcing these standards but did not do so effectively and did not enforce these standards in the informal economy. The Ministry of Labor employs one inspector for each of Guinea-Bissau's eight rural regions and two for Bissau region. The number of labor inspectors was inadequate, and they lacked resources and training. There were no reports inspections were conducted during the year. Penalties, which usually take the form of fines, were not sufficient to deter violations. Many persons worked under conditions that endangered their health and safety. Injuries were common, especially in the construction sector, and safety standards did not apply in the informal sector.